Inner Revolution

Cover illustration by Sebastien Palmieri
Cover photo purchased from *www.shutterstock.com*

Printed in Baltimore, Maryland, U.S.A.
by Grace Printing and Publications,
a ministry of Greater Grace World Outreach, Inc.

ISBN# 978-0-615-72798-1

CONTENTS

PREFACE

Inner Revolution examines our heart before God and His heart toward us. Simple agreement with the nature of who God is creates lasting transformation. Through this life journey of grace we discover and learn the riches of the almighty God. These pages, if taken prayerfully and transparently, could start a revival fire and mission that will consume your life. God has called you to an abundant life!

"A daily glimpse at the Holy One would find us subdued by His omnipresence, staggered by His omnipotence, silenced by His omniscience, and solemnized by His holiness."
– Robert Murray McCheyne

"He who fears God fears no man. He who kneels before God will stand in any situation."
– Leonard Ravenhill

INTRODUCTION

When looking at an iceberg from the surface of the water we can only see a small portion of its essence. When you submerge yourself and examine it, there is substantially more. This is the same with us—the outside shell merely reflects a degree of what is happening on the inside. This inner life is the sanctuary of the heart much like an engine to a car. The outer man must be a reflection of the inner working of the Holy Spirit; in others words, he must live from the inside out. We are not just actors memorizing our lines in a play and going through the motions. This leads to vanity. So much attention is focused on the outer life of behavior and impressions that after a while we lose sight of who we truly are in Christ and Who He is in us. Having the inner man renewed, causes us to live from a perfect resource.

This perfect resource is revealed in Jesus Christ, the God-man. His perfect unconditional love, matchless grace, and unfathomable mercy confronts our depravity and infuses resurrection life in us. This is too wonderful for us to comprehend, it is the brilliance of God's provision. This eternal supply is totally dependant on Him and it will never diminish, regardless of our response. We can be mere spectators or trophies of God's goodness.

The Christian is not made to only survive or just get through life; there is a plan to be revived, a plan to live in our eternal purpose as we walk through the Christ life. When there is no growth or transformation, then we are left to mediocrity. Often troubles stem from a place of boredom and passivity. The inner life produces a radical life which is misunderstood. Some of the first thoughts may be that we have to be fanatical and extreme. However, the true meaning of radical speaks of someone being "close to the source." What definition and contrast this brings, as we are constantly being transformed into another image as we choose to surrender to the plan and process of God's grace. The source that I choose to live from makes a difference. I can experience a limited source where things are counted and calculated or, I can enjoy an inexhaustible source that brings personal revival from the inside out.

Radical grace produces radical change. We can embrace this life that is so freely given to us by God. The starting point is to understand our need. When you hear "need," it is easy to list a lot of "felt" needs—those necessities that engage the human heart to satisfy. But our true need is an absolute relationship. In this writing, when we refer to absolutes and absolute truth we are pointing to and exalting Jesus Christ. Absolutes are those principals established and are unchanging, regardless of biases, situational ethics, or secularisms. Absolutes are perfectly established, explained, and defined by something greater than ourselves and, as a result, they produce healthy changes.

Christ is the greatest example of an absolute and His Truth supersedes reason or debate. Therefore, until we recognize our dire need for His intervention and to be conquered by Him, we remain at the starting line. Pre-salvation indicates that we are going about our way, in love with ourselves and all that surrounds around us. At some point, there is a collision, a confrontation, where what we know and believe is tested and challenged and we are asking the question "why." Our intrinsic dictionary could attempt to translate the why by reasoning, "Do we agree or understand the meaning of what just happened? Do I rely on what I have always believed to get me through again?" The answer to these questions will fuel and interpret my actions and make this a point of opportunity or retreat.

Our inner life is pivotal here. As we think with God, we are able to think through our challenges and have hope. We hear stories of those who make it to the top and their success doesn't bring satisfaction to their true inner core. Their success is exciting, but the identity of a person must be greater than success or failure. Our true need is to be loved, to be valued, and to belong. These touch the inner core of our being. In Christ, we are always accepted, respected, and esteemed. We may not get these things, as often as we would like from people, but this is how Christ handles us all the time.

In the coming chapters, we will unpack these thoughts. God has designed us to be fulfilled and to live in wholeness as we discover and live in our eternal purpose. There are many enemies who want to disturb the inner life and the sanctuary of our hearts. Our need to be always busy may point to a deeper issue. Our need to be stimulated by entertainment or noise or talking says something about us. Why can't we get used to pure silence? The inner life includes a discipline of purposed surrender. We go against the grain of our nature because God wants to impart more; we unplug from all the gadgets and we concentrate and listen to the still small voice of the Lord. Can we sit still for 10 minutes? I have had people say to me, "I can t quiet myself down; there is too much in my head screaming at me."

Sound familiar?

When the inner life is developed, we are able to have a healthy imagination, think objectively and enter into true peace with God. It may take a while to enter into His rest as we cast off the distractions, but Christ is waiting there for us.

We cannot afford to live our lives at the expense of our inner life with God. Depression is on the rise because people are disconnected from hope and their eternal purpose. There is no greater joy than to want what you have, to love what you have, and be satisfied with what you have been given, and to meet God in it all. Contentment is a fruit of the inner life. These pages will address the value of living from the inner core with Christ and discovering and entering into a fulfilled, dynamic life.

Chapter 1
INNER LIFE

For the believer, there is a perfect nature that lives within us, the inner man. The Holy Spirit is an inexhaustible resource and fuels this perfect nature. When we hear that we are seen as perfect, we can raise many reasons to dispute this, but the new man is the perfect nature of Christ within us. Putting this new nature in control of the outer man will cause a chain reaction and bring the amazing grace of God to the smallest of details. The outer man cleaves to the dust; the new man, however, is renewed day by day. This simple choice to yield and have the inward man live as the outer man is crucified with Christ will be life transforming. It is no longer I who lives but Christ.

Living from the inside out is a powerful paradigm shift. We project from the inside out all the time in the way that we think and act. Reactions have been programmed by decisions made and through norms and standards reinforced over time. Only God knows what happens in our hearts and minds. Our language and actions can often mislead others as to what is really happening in our hearts. God sees it all; He sees the motives and the intents. We cannot fool Him. With this knowledge, we may think that Christ's attitude toward us would change due to our moods. But God has chosen to love us beyond all knowledge of our sins, our needs or our shortcomings because He wants to give us something perfect, Himself. This revelation from the inner man can bring health and wholeness to our being.

God's nature never changes; His integrity is solid.

We can know God theoretically through filling our mind with facts and theories, but fellowship with Him as Savior, Father, and friend touches our hearts. Our understanding of who He is brings comfort. We begin to recognize that He is touched with all of our infirmities and went through all things to personally identify with us. As we grasp this, we shift from self being our center, to allowing Christ to be the eternal center, the One in control. The consequence is revolutionary; Wisdom, Peace, Joy, Love, Gentleness, Patience, Meekness are all fruits and qualities that come from this eternal Source. We can generate fragments of these fruits temporarily, but if they are to last they must come from an inner life where God produces real strength. As we believe, embrace, and fellowship with God, these qualities are transferred from the inner man to our outer lives. We then live in the effect and power of these fruits and they govern our hearts, and we begin to thrive.

The human body, which is earthy, is dominated by its five senses. We live to please others and our selves and lose our true self in the process. Behavior and conformity to people's expectations will lead to disappointments and disillusionment because striving to interpret people's expectations will always bring disruptions; we are then left with questions that produce insecurity and restlessness. Often, we miss the purpose in a conflict or situation and become slaves to people. Or, we distance our selves and become as rebels. God desires to reveal inner health in an outwardly unhealthy situation. The places where we don't want to be is often where we need to be to bring spiritual health. The inner life brings God's perfect nature into our mess. We lose our peace and rest the moment we get wrapped up in trying to control outward circumstances that are uncontrollable. Adversity creates stress and anxiety. These outer turbulences can cause inner disruption because adversity is not brought to its proper place—the Altar. Often things in our lives can't be controlled, but we have a choice in how we respond to them—will it be Christ living or me? The difference will be a response or reaction, building something eternal or just doing something to get through the crisis. The outer man's attention is motivated by felt needs, our desire and wants stand at the helm. For example, comfort is a good example of a driving motivation of the outer life; it is so easy for us to consider the path of least resistance to avoid discomfort. The problem with this avoidance mode of thinking is that it creates a stockpile of things to do outside of their proper order. These details crowd our minds, procrastination comes in, and the result is unresolved conflicts that disturb our peace.

The inner man gives us the strength to confront these things, in a healthy fear and trembling. This helps us in the decision-making process on the road toward identifying what we really are designed for and what we need. Being loved by God is our ultimate purpose, as we turn to Him He is looking to be gracious to us. We have important heart questions: What is my purpose? Does what I am doing strengthen my eternal purpose? Will there be a legacy from all this labor? The answers may not come right away, but God walks with us in these moments and, as we turn to Him, we hear the still, small voice of the inner man. Surrendering our chaos to the Lord is a biblical provision; it is given so that we are not crushed by pressures as we cross over the bridge of trying into the realm of trust.

Discovering Christ in the sanctuary of our hearts causes us to be reminded of the eternal realm. The privilege we have is to come into His presence and learn of Him and have newness of life. We find that no one can love us as Christ loves us and nothing in this world can address this cry of the heart. The inner life is the meeting place where we bow before the Lord and receive perfect wisdom and meaning in Him. Picture how you would enter the courts of a king with splendor and majesty all around. Now, imagine the King of Kings within you! Think of perfection magnified to the ultimate degree— this is the sanctuary in our heart in the New Man. In the presence of the Lord, we leave our image consciousness and enter into God consciousness; we then see things as they truly are. It is here where we give the Bible and the Holy Spirit authority that we enter into inner stability and quietness. As we surrender our rights to Christ and He becomes Lord over all, His excellence takes place of our control and we are led by the Spirit. Personal rest and true inner strength are learned and experienced; peace and joy will come back into our lives. Where there is a strong inner life, a communion and embrace of God, the outward circumstances are kept in perspective and emotional scattering is kept at a minimum. Emotional scattering is prevalent as life pulls in so many directions. Our feelings simply demand more of us and for us. God gives wisdom in stillness and quietness to show us where to invest time and energy and where to rest in what has been already given. Because of this contentment, we are insulated from the heat and pressures of life that can easily knock us down. Contentment shows us that Christ has preeminence; therefore what comes out of us is reflecting Christ's nature and not our own. Exercising our will in choosing to have Christ at the center of our hearts and in casting all our cares upon him moment by moment keeps us living in the secret of the inner life.

Amazement is a result of the inner life. The depths of God touch the depths of us and Christ will show us more and more of Himself. His glory will be more evident in everyday moments because we are looking for Him in all things. We will see Him acting and moving in the smallest and greatest of ways. This awareness activates what we know of Him and renews our mind. Worship—or we could say "worth-ship"—elevates the value of why we believe and what we believe. Worship esteems the person of Jesus. We may not always feel like worshipping, but choosing to worship releases Christ in our lives. Worship invites Christ into our moments of life. Worship can produce an eternal value system which brings us back to the nature of who God is—and we learn what He values and we grow in what is important to Him.

Our wonder will build a faith expectation and in worship we will give God the glory that is due. This amazement is a door to deeper meditation as we gaze at perfection. We are constantly reminded that God is not a man that He should lie; He is unchanging and His thoughts toward us are thoughts of peace and not evil. To behold His glory as if we are seeing something so majestic that it takes our very breath away and we are standing in awe—this is worship. We bow down and say, "You are God and I am your loyal subject." This helps us avoid thinking naturally about the supernatural, but keeps things in a sacred perspective. Corruption can derail our inner life; it can pollute through familiarity and calling the sacred things common. Past experience or disappointment can interfere and speak sight's conclusions to our hearts, stealing away the wonder with temporal ideas and we miss the visitation of God. Doubt taints innocent faith, but God in His infinite patience knows this and calls us to Himself even in our double-mindedness. He brings us to the inner chamber and speaks to us an absolute promise and there is personal rebound. We can even worship God in our secular activities, in doing our jobs and running our errands. Details of life reveal who we do these things unto through the attitude we express. Behold God's majesty in the heart and there will no longer be big things or small things—we will stop measuring and enter into moments of worship for He is greater than it all!

Prayer causes intimate connection to God. We first listen and fellowship with who He is and it calms us to concentrate on Him; then we call out to Him and He hears us. Prayer should be more than a time of petition; it is communion with God. We see Christ's broken body and it is bread for us. Remembrance of His spilt blood prompts us to consider His redemption and washes our hearts and minds. This causes worship and we touch the heart of God. Martin Luther wrote that "prayer is the breath of the believer." Without breath there is no continued life. Prayer can be seen as coming to God recognizing who he is and worshipping Him. We bow down in our heart of hearts, we empty ourselves of any personal agenda, and we have come to behold Him. In this heart preparation, receptivity is developed so that we have capacity to hear what the Spirit is saying. Worship also affects our thinking. Things are cleared away so that new thoughts and thought patterns have a place to grow. We are reminded that the purpose of all things is to know Christ and to be loved by Him. Without worship we simply have impersonal knowledge and a perception of God compared to having a personal refreshing relationship with the Savior.

This is the difference between knowing God theologically based on biblical facts or knowing Him personally through a personal impartation in understanding Him closer. As we discover the greatness of God and are aware of His presence, we stand in awe and we are surprised by how good He is. Through such childlikeness, faith renewal comes and we have a new insight that produces understanding beyond facts and draws us into the life of God. Without wonder, our knowledge is limited and reduced to information that does not touch our hearts. Even though we quote Truth from our minds, there is no fire on our inner altar. Libraries of information not applied by faith can result in crystallization or stagnation. We know so much about what to do but we are not empowered to do it. Concepts keep us comfortable in our measured knowledge, but never lead us beyond our selves. This is tragic because if our knowledge doesn't stir us to worship and to personal rhema then pride corrupts us. In humbling ourselves before His mighty hand, we see that no flesh glories in His presence—we agree with absolute truth and we are sanctified. Child-like faith will guard our heart, teaching us to discern what is evil and to love what is pure. In prayer, God reveals the kingdom issues and that He is in control. His designed outcome will eternally be best. Knowing Him is our greatest joy and we will learn His wisdom as we wait on Him.

Much emphasis can be placed on feelings. We can look at our motives and struggle with the reality that we "don't feel like doing" something. Our feelings are fickle and they respond to the good and the bad, so they must follow truth so as not to become the guiding fiction. Feelings are real, but they cloud our sense of the big picture objectively. Absolute truth leads us to worship beyond what we may feel at the moment. Worship brings us to a personal concentration on who He is and what He has completed. This is what feeds our hearts in the true heavenly reality. True worship makes room for what is about to be added in the heart and strengthens our memory to believe again based on Christ's faithfulness. Worshipping in truth protects our propensity for wonder and amazement and increases expectation for more. In the mystery of thankfulness, we simply recognize and enjoy the raw beauty and mystical nature of Christ and His character; He is transcendent and above all, but knowable. He is our friend who stands closer than a brother.

Inner Revolution

Inward change is the catalyst to entering into greatness. Not our greatness, but the revelation of a greatness of another—Christ. As we enter this quiet place, we are never the same. This is our prayer that in His presence, we are changed into His image because of love. God has called us to participate—to come and learn of Him. Change is often approached naturally through another system of dos and don'ts and conforming to idealism. But God makes us a brand new creation in and through His love.

Revolution—the term describes the cause and impact of what we orbit around and this produces radical results. We are changed into the image of what we put at our center; this reality holds, through its force of gravity it brings us up or crashes us down. The impact is the after effect, a mark or legacy to be remembered and to change the course of all who follow. Think of an inner revolution or revival where areas of life that were once inactive are now passionately involved. We may feel as if we are on fire. The wounded are able to love again, the untrusting can choose to be vulnerable and trust again. The unforgiving can release their burdens of self justification and swallow injustice, knowing that Christ is God. He turns the bitter experience to a sweet purpose. This radical change happens through a deeper death where we allow the Holy Spirit to take charge of all of our rights and outcomes. We seek His face the outcome is resurrection life. This is not always a bed of roses, but as we radically rely on the Lord, we become a testimony of the mystery of Christ. Religion doesn't produce revolution because it is based on fairness and man's best efforts. We have to forsake that fairness thinking and our thoughts of justice. Revolution happens as we are changed into the absolute truth that we believe. God brings us to the place of growth where we live in the meaning of what we believe.

Great change happens from the inside out that causes us to live beyond good behavior as we develop "core living." This is living from a place of absolutes; it is real life in real time. Grace is a revolutionary agent because it gives what is needed and not what is deserved. As well as mercy, it takes away what I deserve and gives me what I need—that is powerful! This is the generosity of Christ perpetually to us.

Life is not always clean and neat; it is messy and unpredictable. So to bridge the gap God allows trials to make what we know of Him into that which we live by. For example, we can hear some bad news. The doctor may say that you have cancer and panic strikes, but we have a place of "immunity" in this inner life were Christ and His absolute promises become our refuge and we learn eternal perspectives. Christ turns us from the fear of death, the unknown or loss, and reminds us of our position. We are in the arms of God. Death is a promotion and we are always engaged in preparation for the next life—Heaven.

As our lives revolve around absolutes, life and hope are brought to the most desperate of situations, we go beyond what can be explained and we are comforted.

When all reason and fact point to despair we are carried by another realm, the realm of the promise from the Promiser. We are comforted and encouraged. And the promises build upon one another and we are covered. The momentum of faith takes over and truth in the inward parts preserves us. There are times, of course, when we get discouraged; our eyes put their gaze on something that threatens, but God in His infinite patience He whispers "those whose minds are stayed on Me will have perfect peace". We must not look into the hypnotic trance of reason, but instead embrace the Promiser. Even if it seems as if we are hanging on by a thread, we will discover that He is holding on to us and will never let us go! Those who observe your life see a radical difference, they see an edge. An edge is important because it represents who's side you are on—it defines were you stand. The edge is built through tested decisions that have produced divine experience and wisdom. Risk now is seen as "not what will happen if I do this," but rather "what will happen if I don't do this?" We will be led by still waters even as we walk through the valley of the shadow of death. Christ's rod and His staff will comfort us and correct our erring heart. Faith is our friend for it shows us to the ultimate risk-taker, Christ. Christ's extravagant love, which was shed abroad to us without hesitation, shows us how to function. We begin to take those steps by asking God in this way, "Lord, show me what will glorify you." In our great weakness, God's strength takes inventory of all things for the cause of glorifying Himself.

In the "safe life" mentality, great compromises are made based upon human reason. We may be safe for a season, but because no price was paid in risk there will be no lasting impact. It is in loosing our life; it is not counting it dear unto ourselves to save it; it is in bearing His cross that we exalt all that HE has done. This may seem so paradoxical in a day and age when people pay such a high price for preservation of their selves. Christ more than anyone has showed us that anything of value must be acquired at a price. Jesus was sent for the sole purpose to redeem us at the cost of His very own life. His precious blood is matchless and priceless and was the currency to make us clean—this is revolutionary! Radical grace produces radical change. Anything attainable through our own efforts would be inglorious, but the fact that we cannot save our selves shows us the beauty of His grace so extravagantly bestowed on us. Christ was a revolutionary; One who challenged the system. He knew it was imperfect and broken and He revealed that to us as He walked on this earth. His thoughts and ways are so far beyond us. No wonder He was hated and misunderstood because he was standing against that which was "normal" and smashing concepts with life and glory.

A secure identity brings revolutionary change. We know who we are in Christ and the situation or a person doesn't hypnotize us with a lie! The facts may be stacked up against us, but our identity is in Christ. This changes the way we respond—we don't fight God or people but we trust Him and let God care for people. As we revolve around the absolutes we are kept at peace. With changes happening all around—controlled and uncontrolled—we have capacity to focus and move forward, or we just stand still and see the salvation of the Lord. Think of it; we can survive chaos on the outward with peace in the inner man! This is the desired haven of all of us. We long to be untouchable to the things of the world. We are subject to death and disease and disappointments and the adversity of day-to-day existence can infiltrate our inner core. This happens only by choice. Fear and anxiety are some of the greatest manifestations of a breach in the heart. When we choose to walk by sight, we give authority to that which is lesser and it usurps the greater thing. The Apostle John wrote that "perfect love casts out all fear." Mature love is greater than all fear, all of which is really rooted in self-awareness, so why then do we live in fear? It is because we believe and are more familiar with the lie than we are with the absolute. We understand the lesser because it is what we can calculate and perceive. What robbery! We begin to revolve around the lesser thing and we become prisoners locked in cages of self defeat. But there is hope. The moment we choose to believe and grasp a hold of the absolute promise, we confess it and believe it. This becomes our refuge and

we meet God. It is the place where fire comes down and consumes the natural things of life. In the Old Testament, the people of Israel gathered rocks from the midst of the Jordan River for an altar. God wanted the remnants of the difficulty to be remembered as the people thought of His faithfulness. These stones served as memorials of God's nature and character. He is the present help in time of need. The blood being spilt washes us clean and declares that we are new creations and all things are new. This blood covers us and our lives are consumed with God's glory and acceptance. We are now seen as righteous and perfect.

Without an altar our problems and difficulties will consume us. The lie of trying to manage our sin or guilt will wear out any saint. God's provision is His altar where the guilty are made free and the ashes are removed and beauty is seen.

This altar life results in acknowledging Him, agreeing with who He is and in a spirit of thanksgiving, we give Him preeminence. We learn to surrender all that is of any value and lay it at the feet of Jesus to show Him that nothing is in any competition with Him. We extol and magnify his name—agreeing with Him that He has the sovereign right to act according to His divine purpose regardless of what we want or think we need. In this place of true surrender, there is unspeakable joy and we see the spectrum of God's grace and faithfulness.

At the altar, being conquered (or persuaded) is essential to the exchanged life. We let go of our own ways and we cling to the Almighty. We choose to become a living sacrifice—an offering of praise. Humility, teachability, and willingness are all the results of a surrendered, submitted life that stands in awe of the greatness of God. Our awe leads us to come under the authority of truth and we are moved in the Spirit. As worshippers we continue to stand close to the Master. He begins to shine through our broken vessel. In brokenness, we reveal the true treasure and His life becomes a flow from above.

Satan loves to circumvent this surrender by introducing self awareness. Fear can be one of those common components that try to conquer us when loss seems so imminent. Our emotions speak out of need and potential danger to dictate loss. But there is great freedom in what is left behind. The sacrifice on the altar was tied, and the more it struggled the tighter the ropes clung to the body. More resistance meant more pain. This realization that the animal was powerless in the hands of its captor brought a cease to the struggle and calm was found. As we recognize God's ultimate plan, we stop fighting Him and begin to trust Him, even in the face of loss.

Another powerful deficit motivator that must be surrendered on the altar is the need to stay in control. To think we are able to predict, manipulate and govern every variable that is happening in us and around us is unrealistic. Think of the thousands that needed to be fed while they were with Jesus. The need was great and the resources were small. A young boy offers his lunch—tiny in comparison to the need—and Jesus receives it. He has everyone sit down and proceeds to bless and multiply this lunch to meet and well surpass the needs of the crowd. When we read this story, it is amazing how God comes through in multiplying the seemingly insignificant bread and fish. Naturally to look at such a small resource is almost humorous, but God saw the heart attitude of faith. We have the privilege to be governed by another economy and to give back our heart to the One who knows, sees, and understands all. This means that there is no little thing or no small person or no meaningless resource in the kingdom of God. Whatever is done in faith produces great results.

When we are living in the power of an absolute, our eyes are open to another reality—an eternal reality. We start to see people, places, and things not from a place of possession, but from a place of destiny. Destiny reveals that this situation and its outcome are all for me to be conformed and transformed into a deeper knowledge and life with God. All things are designed to add something to our lives that wasn't there before to make an invisible God visible. From an eternal perspective, I see that I deserve nothing but we have been given all things by God to walk in His destiny. As we offer back what we have been given by God, He will show us the true destiny of why He has given it. People, places, things, problems, successes, and failures have a dynamic to show us Christ and to draw us deeper in our faith. Our destiny or destination unfolds to the measure that we follow the Author and the Finisher, Jesus Christ. In situations, the feeling of teetering or the sense of vulnerability comes in. This may be looked at as insecurity, but this is healthy, because it reveals our need to bring us to a place of absolute surrender and trust. Unknowable variables keep us expectant in the Lord and our expectation and waiting on Him in time reveal tremendous opportunities. Radical reliance on Christ gives us a healthy response. Our cry can be "OK, Lord, what's next? Since nothing happens without Your permission,

I trust You." Our cry can be much different as we rely on ourselves. We can react and fight every detail and be miserable, but there is no exchanged life in that.

The altar life is casting everything on to the Lord, so that we are free to walk in providential liberty. We lay our whole heart and expectation on the altar at His feet. We cast it down so that nothing will be in competition in our thoughts or emotions. We then can love Him with our heart, mind, soul, and strength. Until we do this, we will be double-minded and having one hand on everything rather than completely surrendered to Him. We will never understand the destiny of why things are allowed to enter into our lives until we commit them back to God. This means that we have rest in knowing that the consequences are the Lord's and He knows exactly what we need. Trust is born in these times when Christ carries us and His promise supersedes our words and actions and we rest and operate in His absolute provision. This is fine in theory, but when we are confronted with the option this may not be the first one we pick! With all of our knowledge, we can try to trudge through and make things happen on our own but one thing is lacking—the process of being conformed to the image of His dear Son.

A good illustration can be seen in this picture: we are sitting in the airplane and we have no control of the flight but we see the pilot and trust that he has the experience and skill to take off, fly, and land us safely at our destination. How do we know this? We may look around and see other people's confidence in the pilot and crew, but there will be times when sight is not so clear in producing confidence. We must enter into the faith realm where we commit ourselves to another. As that tin can flies at 36,000 feet, we are being held by another! As the Psalmist often writes, our trust is not in horses or chariots but in the Name of the Lord! We learn to trust in Christ and to rest in His promise that we are being upheld and cared for by Christ. He will never let us go.

In life's challenges, it is possible that we can miss going to the altar. We can carry our pain and not surrender it to the Lord because we may enjoy the attention that it creates. The drama of negative attention can be described as exalting my pain. The secret is surrendering it and saying, "Lord, this is yours." Otherwise, we can begin to fellowship with it and draw an identity from the pain and wallow in the "Why me" complex! Pain can go very deep and can shatter so much of our capacity to receive life from God.

God has a way where pain can show us a new destiny. A nailed scarred, pierced Christ, who endured all manner of troubles, to love us completely wants to carry our pain; He is the Man of Sorrows bearing all our grief so that we are made free. Denial usurps our freedom. We don't deny what has happened, but a way through our pain is releasing the personal injustice of it on the altar. Yes, pain touches all of us; tragedy is no friend. But the destiny of the altar life is that it will bring us to new depth with God. We offer back the unfair situation in our eyes, we look unto Jesus in worship and He consumes our offering and leads us through. Maturity is developed, discernment is realized and empathy for others is cultivated as we learn Christ. A ministry can be born in you! Fairness must be relinquished and not used as a crutch or measuring tool. It is true: it seems to us that God is not fair. But remember, He is just and does all things from the place of eternity. One day, when we are with Him we will know all things. This is a paradigm shift in our thinking. Under the natural mind's reasoning, we do good for God and He does good for us. I scratch your back; you scratch mine. There is no growth in this—everyone is comfortable, but without a death there is no new life. Christ promises to always be near in these times and lovingly lead us to Himself. . It is impossible to know what will happen next but we can fellowship with timeless truth and rest in this place of vulnerability and be transparent in intimacy and have our ashes exchanged for something eternal.

"The altar—the lonely place were I lay my burdens down. There, my foolish heart finds sanctuary. Stillness and calm capture my heart as I lay down my self and in death resurrected life begins".

His Conquering Presence

Our will to fight is intrinsic; we are all made to fight or to take flight. We need wisdom to know how to fight for the right things, or we will be conquered by the wrong things. Destructive thought patterns and self-absorbed habits creep in if our lives are not surrendered at the altar. We will choose our own way with self at the center and our focus will be led astray. But God is always with the believer, He is present. We may not discern the power of this presence, but it is there ready to manifest God's eternal purpose. As we grow in grace and knowledge of Jesus, we store timeless truths in our memory centers through faith. In rehearsing what we know about who God is, we can experience the manifestation of His presence. This knowledge is more than just facts; it becomes a tool that can be called on in a crisis or need. A "guiding fiction" can sometimes bring us into confusion. However, our perspective can be changed and we become aware that we are not alone and that with God we are a majority. Our human designs fade in His presence. We move from an attitude of trying to save our self to discovering His will and purpose. We begin to understand that God is bigger than anything that we face and His presence conquers our doubts.

Our arsenal of grounded, resident knowledge is so important because this helps correct and create the way we talk to ourselves. This "self talk" moves our will to choose the right things according to an objective belief system. What we tell ourselves as we do what we do is important to the longevity of our action. If we are critical and full of self-analysis, we will sabotage ourselves and not see the good when it comes. But we can re-assess and examine our hearts, taking inventory for encouragement for we know this: greater is He who is in us than He who is in the world. Our almighty, All-knowing, Omni-active, everywhere present God is with us! What could compare? If self-preservation is at the center, then God is seemingly dwarfed in the light of the threat. If we discover His presence and worship Him, we will see the true reality. Our "Self Talk" must be derived from the throne of Grace.

In our situations, we can have many different types of influences. As we function in our different arenas, we learn to give authority to the right influence. In conflict, there is a confrontation of these different influences. What we think could be very different from what is actually happening. With a spiritual perspective, we operate from absolutes rather than living in reaction. A ricochet can happen if we just live in cause and effect. Fatalistic thinking— "what will happen, will happen"—can really inhibit our motives. The resources of our inner life provide understanding so we can initiate the kingdom of God and give authority and attention to the spiritual aspects of our situation. As faith is spoken, we see God's wisdom. If we have the right content within our hearts, our actions will not be reactions but responses. One reaction can be retaliation without thought, but a proper premeditated response sees the true need of the recipient and addresses it in love. This is spiritual reflex, a trained response. We respond by addressing the need and not the symptom. We become bridge-builders rather than the person with the hammer making more of a destructive mess. With a revelation of how much we are loved and forgiven personally, the reflex will be to freely give to others. If I ponder what this person means to me, his value and my love from him becomes the content of my response. I fellowship with who that person really is in context to the overall picture, rather than just zeroing in on one situation or mistake. Our tunnel vision turns to a bird's eye view of the big picture. This objective thinking leads us in spiritual reflex and we give authority to those aspects that move ourselves and others toward maturity. When this inner life has control, the ability of truth becomes the umpire of our souls; it will identify and call out those things in our heart for what they really are. It discerns the fruitful and the harmful. As we invest in our heart health, we will see things clearer.

As we get to know absolute truth and the favor that is on our lives, we will express these things to others. This is a growing process, the inner life takes us to a place where Another lives through us and for us for a greater destiny. No longer do we need to fight for justice or personal vindication. Instead, we choose to be a victim, to lift up the life of Christ. Our responses reveal whether we are running on empty or if we are partaking of a limitless source. A limitless source is Christ's love for us. Here, we have rest and reveal temperance not tolerance. With life's demands, we can run ourselves down caring for everyone else's needs without having balanced thinking in our hearts and minds. Emotional scattering can bring withdrawal, implosion, and explosion. We can be stretched in so many directions emotionally that we forget the most important thing and that is to live from a divine source. A person who is stretched beyond measure and neglecting his core will have misery. This describes much of our society today, so many are running after things that won't last and are really decorations in the house of life.

Through surrender to the right Person in our lives, we learn to be aware of His presence in worship with no intimidation. In his book "The Place of Immunity," Francis Frangipane writes:" Before we can truly discern the presence of God, we must recognize the gentle blowing that precedes His presence. What is this spiritual phenomenon? It is the Holy Spirit subduing the activities of the earth for the Lord's approach. If we attain the power needed at the end of this age, we must learn to detect, without great signs, the whisper of God's wind. He will not fight for your attention; He must be sought. He will not startle us; He must be perceived. It took no special skill to discern the earthquake, the fire or the great storm. But to sense the gentle blowing of God, our other activities must cease. In our world of great pressures and continual distractions, the attention of our

tions and stimulants. We cry out in transparency and are naked before the living God. He sees our poor and bankrupt spirit in need of Him and He fills us. We hold on to nothing but Christ, and at that point we begin to discover the meaning of what we know. We go beyond the mere intellectual fragments we may have collected. The desire is to live in the power of what we know with inner stability and poise. We cross the line from talking about things into the Holy Spirit's transference of a ministry. No longer do we just talk, but we operate from inside what we are in—this is living from our core. Forgiveness no longer just a word, it is a revelation with response; we have seen the amazing mountain of offenses that we have been forgiven of so therefore we forgive. He who has been forgiven much, loves much. When there is this pouring out of the heart, there is no longer a desire to impress people, we begin to live for the audience of One.

The manifestation of Christ's life is unparalleled. He held nothing back from His Father. He was in total submission to His will. All that he did was in unity with His father's will—He was poured out. This is a beautiful secret. Instead of living with a personal agenda, Christ expressed His Father's heart. Submission is a secret to power. We come under the healthy authority of someone and learn his heart and become a covering to others in that same authority. This life that we come under is transferred to our family and situations—and Christ's life reigns. By willingly coming in glad surrender, we open the gate for the Holy Spirit to move because we are out of the way. The apostle Paul often called himself "the prisoner of the Lord." He saw himself as the Lord's bond-servant. His life was at the mercy of another. This has great value because the apostle Paul was not serving only in the strength of himself, but he was endowed with the life and power of another. He represented Someone greater than him. This is how ordinary people do extraordinary things.

Chapter 3
DEVOTIONAL LIFE

When worship has completely enraptured our attention, God speaks a personal word. This is "devotional life". He ministers to the inner man and rhema replaces mere knowledge. The practice of worship prepares our hearts to hear from God. Rhema speaks of the moments when the veil comes off our eyes and we see a glimpse of the meaning and glory of the absolute. These personal words inspire great motive, energy, and drive to pursue God and His purpose. It is one thing to read something from an author and quite another when you know the Author and He addresses you by name and directs the text to you! We discover His devotion to us and it inspires us. He is passionate about us and we discover that He needs nothing in this world, but He wants us involved in a fellowship—what a mystery. The more attention we give enables us to catch a clear glimpse of what the Author is saying and we discover His heart. The longevity of our ministry and our faith is caused by the state of wonder and amazement toward Christ. This revelation will be fresh in us and our life will not only be changed, but exchanged into something brand new! We will leave just conformity and enter into transformation. What's happening? Our inner life is being poured out and affecting our outer life with a personal word from God for those we are in contact with.

Restlessness can come in when we have things in our lives that are not addressed with a word from God. They can be unresolved conflicts; or, in the rule of punctuation they are like a dangling participle. Restlessness is quelled as we rehearse the greatness of the Absolute. This is worship—giving authority to the right things in our lives; these things promote health. This is not to be confused with "clearing of the mind,' which is suppressing recognizable thoughts. This is common practice where we force thoughts out of our minds rather than confronting them and speaking to them and letting truth dominate them. God's plan is that we cast our cares upon Him; we are to totally hurl them onto Him so He can carry them. We are not to take them back. The beautiful mystery here is that when we are free from the burden, we are able to think clearly. Maybe physically things haven't changed, but no longer are we fighting for control. We now are students and learners of Christ and He is showing us how to navigate through. We are refreshed with a perspective that looks beyond roadblocks and "through" situations. God speaking to us gives birth to hope and we are deeply encouraged.

Hope is a confident assurance that what we are facing will have an end and meaning. Hope is precious because without it we enter into despair and we spiral into negativity. Hope is this: knowing that someone greater has the reins and He is attentive to respond when called to act. Hope is the fruit of quietness which produces a deep rest. It produces receptivity and my ears are open and my heart is willing. Trust is born in these moments, and we receive and abide in health because we are connecting with the core of the matter rather than with the distractions. This right belief core dictates to neutral emotions which respond and control right behavior. These emotions which are not designed to think and lead are now able to be led and to respond in health.

thoughts are those that produce life and capacity—they are building blocks. Even in the most trying situations we can tower with right thinking rather than cower in fear. If we are drinking from the right resource, we will be sustained in hope and Christ will replace our guiding fictions. The inner stability that is produced by right thinking affects every aspect of our lives. Our decisions and our conversations are transformed into spheres of expectation and confidence. How we interpret information is important, to organize our knowledge into a proper inventory reduces clutter in our souls. "What we know" is organized through meditation and becomes active as a guard at our heart's door. We pass from knowledge to life. We live in the meaning rather than just the forms. Trials are designed to bring us over this threshold. However, our flesh often fights God and the process takes longer. God's plan is that we experience what we know. Even the simple word "I love you" heard deep in our heart could chase fear and produce tremendous inner strength. Living in the meaning of those words would heal so many intimacy disorders and produce deep inner peace. We will do what we believe; therefore meditation on what we have received situates what we know in the right place. Now, we think and come to the right conclusions. Life in the definitions only is not enough! We have all accumulated information and it is easy to spout off words and give the appearance that we know what we are talking about. It is living in the meaning that causes the power of what I know to be governed by Who I know. We avoid pious platitudes and there is a genuine response of grace and wisdom. We are changed and those around us are affected.

Inner strength goes way beyond natural strength

or talent; it comes through living from the inside out in meditation, reflection, and communion. Meditation brings resident knowledge of an absolute truth or promise to the forefront of our minds. We begin to fellowship with the Promiser. Here comes the revelation of the building blocks of why we believe what we believe. We ponder and muse and enter into the mood of what we know and possess. We become possessors rather than mere professors. It is easy to talk a good game, but when the rubber meets the road what we really possess will be made evident.

As meditation progresses, reflection is produced and we begin to examine and learn personally what we have stored in our hearts. We begin to scrutinize and examine knowledge as though our life depended on it. This in turn creates Rhemas—a personal revelation from God for our lives. To the measure that we "unpack" and relearn truth will be to the measure that our recall will release power. Reflections bring us into the image of what we are mediating on. God is faithful to show personal wisdom to the student who takes the time to seek Him. Often we can battle with being a steward of time. Our schedules are packed with demands, but the value of the treasure cannot be told as we invest in reflecting on God's personal word. Inner stability and the navigation of life are found here.

Time is precious; we can never really manage time, but we can recognize priorities. Priorities are like maps that enable us to choose the best way to use this gift of time. Rehearsing what God has shown you will create a respect and anticipation for more learning. For instance, the archeologist carefully removes the dirt to unveil buried treasures. There is no hurry lest they damage or disturb the relic. It takes finesse to preserve mystery and lead us into true discovery and true meaning. As meaning is discovered, we honor the knowledge that we have received and we recognize it for what it truly is. In reflection, we learn to slow down and let the words sink deep into us rather than rushing through to complete a task. Saturate yourself in the majesty of God and discover the truth.

Communion is the consequence of the first two secrets mentioned—meditation and reflection. The outcome of what meditation and reflection produces causes newness of life from an eternal source. As we break the bread and drink the wine figuratively speaking, we enter into His life, according to John 6:63. We believe and trust in the provision of Jesus and His broken body becomes our food and we are fulfilled and satisfied with a new identity. The wine is significant representing the blood which washed away our sins. As we receive Christ's new life as our sustenance, we are converted. We believe in the Absolute in spite of what evidence we see; we begin to take on the identity of the Absolute by faith and live in the effects of a new life produced beyond ourselves. Through communing with God, our communication is transformed and there is radical change. This change can be seen because we are thinking and interpreting the things that we see differently rather than just by sight. There is now a new dimension, one that is objective. This exchange of life teaches how to delight in grace.

Communion greatly affects our identity. My identity is what I tell myself that I am from analyzing the facts that have been acquired in my belief system. When our identity is established in the right place, we define and be convinced and persuaded and transformed for His Glory.

Interior Power

God's glory is our hiding place. The shadow of the Almighty covers us and these places where we can't be touched or disturbed are places of immunity. Here, we find security and total protection. There is safety and privilege. We enter in, kick our shoes off, and rest our weary souls. Externals drift away into the distance as we open our ears to our heavenly Father. We enter into the comfort that every aspect of our lives is in the control of Another who is infinitely stronger and wiser than ourselves. Our heart doesn't have to be disturbed as we enjoy communion with the Father. When Jesus was in the boat during the storm, He was asleep. He was in faith-rest because He knew the Father and the Father's care for Him. His disciples panicked and disturbed His rest, but even then He had wisdom on what to do because He was not "under" the situation but was "over" it, thinking with the Father. Panic happens when fear is leading the way; the heat of the situation dehydrates us spiritually. We may wander from our refuge, but the refuge is always available. A choice to look unto Christ and put on the armor of absolute truth will bring us back to the place of safety. His provision will protect us from the fiery javelins of the devil. This covering is available through a relationship of trust in which we can take steps of faith with the great hope of learning who Christ is

This place of immunity produces power. Power is more than just might and advantage. Power is influence. This influence is God's presence in us declaring

Recognizing the reality that we can't do it is liberating, and we take that knowledge to the inner chamber of our hearts. We cry out to God. He loves us and shares with us an established truth about ourselves and the situation. He assumes His role in our situation and we have a new outlook. Without humbling ourselves and seeing our need, we trudge along with a plastic smile as we go through the motions. This could lead to withdrawal and forsaking all that we hold dear. The ambition and pride of man often keeps from seeing our weakness, the arena of reliance, the place of power! Naturally, we don't want people to see us as weak; rather, we want to exhibit the image of competence and control. What we need to do is fall down on our knees and pour out our hearts before the living God and listen humbly as He teaches us, loves us, and endows us with power and inner stability.

This place were we relinquish control is the place of power and health. Instead of our soul becoming fragmented, it is unified in the Absolute because we have agreed and taken our rightful place of expectation.

We can't do this all in our own strength and intellect. There needs to be the release of the ministry of the Holy Spirit. As we come to Jesus and relinquish control, we begin to learn the true meaning of life. This process of submission is pivotal to power. We often manipulate our outcomes because we are clever, but we never tap into the fullness that is in our interior life with God. We discover purpose and power and meaning. Purpose is to not only exist, but to be a part of something greater than ourselves and impact the lives of others because our days are numbered. Power is our privilege to initiate the right things that will produce life. Even restraint is a form of power, because even with the privilege we at work and to lean on Him. God's answer is far beyond us and greater than we think. God's delays are not his denials. When we bow our knee to Him, angels are commissioned. A man who has intimacy with God is not intimidated by people and situations. Don't give Him the silent treatment today—pour out your heart for He is waiting to hear you. You have all of Heaven with you—release its power through prayer!

Stillness comes when we are dominated by the Holy Spirit in truth. Domination can be a fearful word depending on our perspective. But we become still when we realize that something greater is present with us. For instance, we walk through the forest, our feet move over the crushed pine needles; the beauty of nature is all around, the wind softly sighs through the trees, we can take a deep breath and close our eyes and feel as if we are part of the forest. This stillness can be achieved physically and mentally through willpower, but let's go deeper into something more substantial. We must enter into the next step which is quietness—harmony in the Spirit. Not only must we agree that something or someone is greater than our selves, we must submit to that greatness and have it permeate our whole being. An orchestra with so many parts is led by one—the conductor. Each person has their instrument and part to play. With the wave of the baton, the conductor leads the orchestra alive in musical symmetry that ignites the soul. There are many facets of sound acting as one entity. When quietness comes in, we have made ourselves vulnerable to the Absolute, and now the consequence is that we have peace passing through our being proving and releasing the truth. A noisy soul, contrarily, is easily disturbed and agitated. Things from the past and worries about the future hijack the present. Restlessness stirs the desire to act without the wisdom of how God is moving. Scattered actions in many directions are taken without the determination of our core need. Restlessness thrives as we struggle for control that is fleeting; we tend to fixate on something in our past that we have no power to change. Our focus and concentration direct our minds and hearts into that which we interpret as important. What we reward with time and energy will bear fruit —good or bad. We must ask ourselves "what produces life and what doesn't"? This will be a deciding factor for healthy thought patterns.

Chapter 4
THE EXCHANGED LIFE

The desire of our hearts is that we would no longer live but that Christ would live in us and through us. This is the great exchange of power and true life. We bring our hearts to the altar of God. Gripping the edges of the altar in reverence, we see the true nature of sacrifice. Positioned with care, the fire consumes the offering in satisfaction. Then standing in worship, discovery begins in the fear of the Lord as His fire burns within our hearts. Let us release those precious things that detract from the fervent flame and put them into the hands of Jesus and He will be the divine caretaker and protector of our souls.

The Bible illustrates; "And Manoah said unto the angel of the LORD, What is thy name, that when thy sayings come to pass we may do thee honor? And the angel of the LORD said unto him, Why askest thou thus after my name, seeing it is wonderful. So Manoah took a kid with a meat offering, and offered it upon a rock unto the LORD: and the angel did wondrously; and Manoah and his wife looked on. For it came to pass, when the flame went up toward heaven from off the altar, that the angel of the LORD ascended in the flame of the altar. And Manoah and his wife looked on it, and fell on their faces to the ground." (Judges 13:17-20)

These are amazing verses. We see that the offering was given to the Lord by faith and He received it! The fire was God's way of consuming the offering for His glory. Fire is revealed in the Bible so many different ways. It speaks of judgment, passion, the presence of the Lord and a light for the way through, to name a few.

We use fire to cook raw things. If left alone and out of control, fire can become a destructive force. The Holy Spirit is called the "Spirit of burning." We see in many examples where the Spirit was manifested when the vessel was clean and prepared—there would be a fiery demonstration. Fire reflects the holiness of God cleansing the vessel and making it worthy for the Master's use. The starting point is the fear of the Lord, where we honor and revere the Master in entirety. His life falls and consumes our dross and the fire burns until the Master's face can be clearly seen. The fire touches and impacts all that it comes in contact with. If we were to take precious metals and put them in the flame, they would return to liquid form to be shaped and fashioned for use as utensils, tools or weapons. The blacksmith who forges a blade employs great heat, the pressure of his hammer, and the anvil to craft a sword for battle. Fire is the means of reducing the metal to its purest form so that it can be remade into something useful.

The Spirit of burning is when we share the same passions that Christ had through the manifestation of the fruit of the Holy Spirit. We learn what He loves and what He hates. Our motivations are then fueled through His passions and we rest in what we are doing even with great activity. Passion is so much more powerful than zeal. We see zeal as an emotional spurt that often tires and burns out; passion, however, represents an ongoing flame where His cause is fueling our hearts. It is more than activity; it is our life's mission. We learn the burden of God and urgency is born. No longer do we rely on time as an inexhaustible source, but we have learned to number our days and incline our hearts to wisdom.

This life from above comes down like fire when we live in the meaning of what we know and believe in. Often, we see the ease of accumulating knowledge, but it is very different to live in the power or result of that knowledge. As the Holy Spirit illuminates our eyes and opens them to new mysteries, our hearts are ignited. This is far greater than an emotional experience, certainly we are responding to the magnificence of God—but this is a slow burn that increases in temperature and fervency. As God touches our heart and we are illuminated in an area that once was cold, we begin to discover a new reality. We see the Author behind the words. We see the One who fulfills all the Law behind the work. We see the risen Christ! Until we have crossed this threshold, we will have polished words but no real power.

Power is the ability to choose life and function in liberty without being held captive. We then begin to experience the meaning behind the word. Physical strength and might show advantages, but true power comes from exhibiting my true identity. Power can be demonstrated through restraint, weakness, and even failure. As the Spirit's fire consumes and cleanses our vessel, we grow deeper in intimacy and Christ's life is reflected. We discover a quality of might that is sourced in the fire from the altar. The Holy Spirit fills us.

Our yearning for the Spirit of burning is best described in the following prayer:

"Heavenly Fire fall down and consume me.
Burn fervently the cold wastelands of my heart.
The waxing cold and the dross ignite with your Fire
And create an inner Fire that shows me all of Thee.

More of Thee and less of me,
Burn, oh, glorious flame from heaven's Altar".

As we behold this mystery of godliness, God inspires us with His love; a love that doesn't demand a change but produces one through His power. Our submitted will releases God's power and inspiration is ignited. The breath and flow of the Holy Spirit takes us to new places. God's breath of inspiration leads to illumination where there is no obstruction of the flesh. We see and hear things with the inner ear and truth penetrates our hearts in action. We begin to blaze and burn with a new value system that leads us to a fulfilled core life. We continually place wood on our altar through faith obedience; so that we are consumed in inspiration. Our expectations now are no longer sourced in ourselves or our behavior, but are laid down in absolute adoration to know Him in this mystery and we begin to burn. God reveals what He has placed in our hearts; something that we didn't produce and we become governed and led by something greater. We are captivated by His life and this labors through us in our ministry to the world.

Lasting Change — Submission

Think of the freedom of our will and how God works through our right to choose. We, in our free thinking, are often blinded by needs and desires and feelings. God, in His great wisdom, created us to have a free volition so that we could follow Him and choose because of love. When we relinquish control to Him and come under the authority of God's Word, we are then led by the Spirit in peace, power, and provision. Change happens as we yield to Him.

Change is seen through transference; in other words, we allow the life of another to control or influence our own. Transference happens on many levels even down to something as basic as our countenance. People perceive or interpret things according to their own understanding, but what we project reveals what kingdom we are communing with. For instance, in times of loss or disillusionment, someone may bring comfort. An embrace or a kind word touches the heart and you're carried for a moment and your pain is not so acute. Another example is forgiveness, releasing someone from the consequence of his trespass and giving what is needed and not what is expected. This is liberating; this is transference. Imagine a life lived heart to heart; spirit to spirit.

It can go the other way as well. A violent act or a crime, could lead to the transference of fear or anxiety, wondering if it could happen again or happen to me. This is why we have civil servants that have structures of securities to give the impression of safety. The fear of the Lord keeps us from the terror of evil. This change happens when there is an embrace of divine transference. The drug addict loses the identity of his habit and embraces a new identity, a fresh language and a transformed self-image. We are no longer what we once were, we are now new creations!

True satisfaction brings lasting change, which really comes from an "exchange." I surrender my thoughts and ways to embrace divine Absolutes that create a new way. Often, we don't see it this way. We see that if we can get what we want, then our needs will be met. This way of life deceives us because we cannot see the whole picture of God's plan. We really don't know our true needs, our wants are temporary and shortsighted to the "now" life. We know what we want, but God aims to meet our deep needs. We can be blinded by the crises and demands of today so that we don't really know how to prepare for the changes of tomorrow. Even if we are fortunate enough to get all that we want, the heart hungers for more. Why is that? Because satisfaction is when our souls are content in an Absolute and we have laid our lives down on the altar of God. Then, nothing is in competition with Him and we live for Another. This exchanged life is Christ and all of HIS fullness pouring out of a willing vessel without any obstructions. Finally, our thirst is quenched. The world and its vices leave the soul even thirstier with only the promise of water to quench the thirst but no delivery. We were designed for God, for the eternal life that is fulfilled in Him.

Certain stimuli tantalize us and tempt us to conform our behavior. The knee-jerk reactions to stimuli will weary us because we start and stop multiple times and, after a while, we say "this doesn't work" and give up. Our provision for lasting change however, comes from a new heart, to allow truth to be stored up in our hearts and minds. This action of investing time in our selves through hearing, reading, and meditating bears great fruit.

Absolute truth is activated and takes over the "driver's seat" the moment we believe it. We say "yes" and Absolute truth begins to take us for the ride of our lives. A relationship of trust guides us rightly. As we trust and believe, the truth will begin to lead us. As we have said earlier, surrender puts us in a place were we would not normally choose and we embrace something that we would not naturally embrace and we experience a metamorphosis. We are transformed into another image that is made after true holiness. For example, someone maybe addicted to drugs. Through becoming part of an accountability group, he learns that he is not his sin. He had embraced destruction. The way back is to feed health into his thinking so he can develop a change of mind that will lead to a change of actions. The reinforcement of life from the truth moves the mindset; allowing destiny and hope to stir value-system changes. Choices made to embrace life expose lies and, thereby, hope is realized.

The natural mind often wants to analyze and solve problems, but this exchanged life means we are no longer our own! This is pivotal—we are not our own we are bought with a price! This affects our whole way of thinking—we begin to seek the thoughts and heart of the One we serve before we give preference to our own ways. We seek to understand rather than to be understood. We can spend so much time trying to make ourselves clear when in actuality if we listen and observe, we begin to understand what is truly important. This is when lasting change begins.

Chapter 5
A BEAUTIFUL MIND

A spiritually healthy heart dictating to our mind is essential for effective change. This invisible world between our earlobes is a world that few know outside of our selves. This private life we don't even know in its entirety because it is fleeting. It is possible to be present physically but have our minds on another planet, daydreaming about those things that have captivated our attention. Our imagination is designed to be a launch pad for expressing faith and creativity. It could be called a "Genesis Room" a place of creative thought and inspiration that embraces the invisible possibilities. Satan through polluting our imagination causes a dumb-ing down of the mind through fantasy. His plan is to pollute the mind and stimulate corrupt actions. He creates false images that stunt creative growth and rob the present reality. We have the "right now". Actually, now just passed by—what did you do with that moment? There went another one. It just passed by. What did we think and act upon in these moments? True reality is now, how do we handle our "now" with Christ? Now may not be what we want or where we want to be, but it is our present reality. We accept it and allow the momentum of our good decision to be realized. God has given each one a tremendous destiny that can only be realized in faith. As we meditate and reflect on Christ, the Holy Spirit empowers us to imagine the impossible and take steps, hand-in-hand, with the Him to do it!

Imagination

Imagination can be a very subjective topic. We are the product of our thoughts—as man thinks so he is. Our thoughts can be innumerable about a certain subject and when we have been convinced action follows. In knowledge, there is tremendous power to create, to destroy, to encourage, to discourage, etc. We think and choose to be a part of, or not be a part of, something and so on. What we feed and internalize and listen to has a direct connection to our actions and our physical body. When we think about imagination, we see the many avenues where it can run wild. Consider entertainment. Other people's lives and decisions are scripted and presented for observation. The humor and the pain experienced feed our memory centers with perceptions. We can relate to these false worlds and often vicariously live through what we watched on TV or on the movie screen. We allow our memories to carry us back with fondness or regret to other days and create invisible scenarios to walk through.

Imagination is powerful. Imagination is the immaterial world of imagery that through impulses of the mind can project ideas and suggestions for our will to consider and act upon. We cannot hold our imagination in our hands, but through hundreds of thoughts we can create an intangible "reality." This reality programs our mind for action. Sure, reason sometimes does get in the way before action is taken. Still, this process goes on in minds and hearts, generating perceptions and stirring passions.

The five senses greatly affect our imagination. Tastes, touches, smells, sights, and sounds fuel the processes of our knowledge on a natural level. Often vivid memories of people, places, and things lost in our history can be triggered through our senses. It is like a movie in our mind bringing us back in the "fragrance of memory" to things that brought us great joy or great pain, we feel as though we have entered a time warp and our emotions carry us along to the outcome.

Imagination is a beautiful gift that Christ has given. It is a chamber in our mind filled with good and precious treasure. It can provide a map to help us make decisions in faith; we see that faith is the evidence of things hope for and the confidence of those things not yet seen. This shows us that faith is the bridge between imagination and decision. Think of the kid who spends his childhood imagining playing baseball and hitting home runs. Finally, he joins a team to learn and train in all the aspects of baseball. One day he stands at the plate and anticipates the pitch he has already seen coming in his mind for years. The imagination and action come together as he takes his swing. Now it may not always work out that the swing results in a big hit, there could be a strikeout. This is very possible and we have all experienced the many sides of disappointment. But the success in this story is not that the boy hit the home run or that he struck out, it is that he stood at the plate with anticipation and preparation! He stood up and he was accounted for. He followed though and saw his imagination lead to reality. Obviously, time, training, and investment help us in the pursuit of our dreams. Then, we must go and be present in the arena. Not everything in life will happen in safe, predictable areas and ways, for risk is a primary ingredient in any creative venture. Our threshold of risk will be determined by the conclusion of our imagination. A painter steps before a blank canvas and in his mind's eye he sees what he will do. The strokes will come and are led by what is rooted in his imagination. Masterfully, he puts upon the canvas the beauty he has in his heart. A motivation to create overrides the risks he perceives. Something inside him tells to go, to show up, and to take hold of his destiny. A healthy imagination processes everything as an opportunity; an opportunity to embrace reality and become stronger and wiser.

We are not talking about mind over matter. We don't want to mislead or cause a person to live in the denial of reality. Someone may have a severe illness -- even one that is fatal—and think that an active imagination is the key to his healing. He strives to focus his energy into the "channel" of wellness, ignoring the reality and instruction of his physician. Yes, God can and does heal according to His divine purpose. However, our relationship to the Lord should be one so deep that we accept the realities of His providence and sovereignty for our lives. We can choose to enter into a new destiny with him in facing the challenges, the successes, and the pains he allows.

What will we do with what has been dealt to us? How will we think about it? We may think that we are being punished or have made a mistake or we have missed something, but in all truth there are no accidents. God has foreordained our lives with a purpose in all things. This is what the prophet talks about in Isaiah, "treasures in darkness". In the most unexpected places, we find the greatest lessons for this life and the one beyond. We realize the true treasure is to know Christ; this is even more precious than deliverance.

have seen. Then, we can reconsider the options that are before us. This process happens in crucial moments, but the outcome of these invisible calculations affects our realities. What we ponder on becomes who we are and defines where we are going.

Fantasy

When considering fantasy, we have to recognize it as the powerful agent it is. In our world today, there are multitudes of temptations, avenues of alternate realities that provide ways of escape. These ways can come to occupy the deep recesses of our hearts. Often, we turn to these in order to tolerate present miseries or just to deal with common familiarity and boredom. Fantasies are a false reality that is enabled by the ego because of desire motivated by disappointment or disillusionment. Fantasies can take the imagination hostage by projecting "best-case scenarios" that are extreme and unreachable. For this reason, fantasy represents the ultimate foe of a healthy imagination. These vain, empty imaginations could be described as seemingly harmless detours off of the "high" way God leads along. Detours, however, can be dead-end streets. Aimlessness can come in where we pursue false realities as though they are attainable. Fantasy omits the negatives of the scenario and it constructs idealistic, alternative realities to mask the truth of our situations. Fantasy tends to lead the self in ways of gratification at the expense of developing meaningful exchanges with others and intimacy with God. We may fool ourselves into thinking our fantasies are not hurting anyone, but there is such blindness in this thinking. The more we replay the fantasy in our minds the more "real" it can become to us. Alterations then come to the way we think about ourselves, about others, and about our situations. Precious time and opportunities are lost in these holding patterns. A turtle could fantasize about being a hare, dreaming of how he would spurt through life with speed and agility. Perhaps, the turtle lusts for the popularity and recognition the hare receives because of his ability. The fact remains, however, that the turtle is a turtle. He was made for a purpose with a certain ability to perform. As the turtle dreams about being fast and furry, he loses a proper sense of self and sets himself up for disappointment. He may talk like a hare, act like a hare, and even try to think like one but he will never be one.

True Reality

Inspired imagination is based in a true reality that encourages outrageous thoughts. These thoughts are based on a faith that moves us to glorify God with our heart, soul, mind, and strength.

Show up! I can still here these words ringing in my ears. "Show up, and the rest is up to God!" These words have been a kick in the pants many times in the face of procrastination. We must embrace our realities. This means we are 100 percent committed to where we are. We live in the NOW life. It is easy to live from event to event or from happy instance to happy instance, but we greatly sacrifice the NOW.

Often, pain inhibits our desire to embrace today. How we interpret what is happening to us helps us perceive the end of the matter. Reality is what is "real," what is happening now. It is easy to drift and be 20 percent present and 40 percent in the past wanting to change something unchangeable and 40 percent thinking of how the future will be different. This can really lead us into confusion and irritation. Accessing truth helps us to navigate through the good and the bad. All things pass, and all things also work together for good to them that love God and who are called according to his purpose. In all things, we learn something for the next step of life. We can be in that state of mourning with our loss seeming larger than life; but in God's economy nothing or no one is replaced. We have people and things for seasons and once they have fulfilled their purpose they are removed and in eternal rotation God gives his best again.

Being real with our family, our selves, and our world is the doorway to fulfillment. Honesty before God can clean our warehouse and make room for real life and real fulfillment. In talking with a blind man recently, he shared with me "I concentrate on that which I can do and not on what I cannot do." This simple statement is profound. Yes he is blind—that is reality—but he looks at his disability not as an excuse but as an opportunity to get up again and reach out. Whatever seeming deficiency we may be experiencing, God uses all things with an eternal purpose for his glory. Consider the opportunity before this blind man. What identification he chooses to tap into, to touch and minister! Our infirmities and disabilities help us enter in to the world of identification with others –this is a profound reality.

As we close these meditations, my prayer is that you would know that you have an eternal destiny prepared for you! Destiny is Life we haven't experienced yet, but this Life is planned. It is something amazing that we will progressively discover. As we shift and embrace the truth of who we really are in Christ and embrace the Inner life, Altar life and the Devotional life, we will discover more and more of Christ. Life is an adventure of faith, what a privilege to reveal Christ to a lost and dying world as a trophy of His grace.

"We desire, dear Lord, that Thou shouldest be more to us than Thy work. It is not enough for us to plough Thy fields or keep Thy sheep, we want to serve Thee most of all. Help us to keep Thee in view all day, and whatsoever our hands find to do, may we do it in love to Thyself." -FB Myer

MEDITATIONS AND MUSINGS

Please enjoy these timeless truths as resources of this book. Each meditation represents the notes of what is written. May God keep unveiling his majesty to you!

Meditations – 1

Sanctuary – The holy place of Sanctification set apart unto God—Exodus 3:3-5

Ezekiel 7:22 – "they shall pollute my secret [place]"…

Psalm 91:1 – "He that dwelleth in the secret place of the most High shall abide under the shadow of the Almighty".

1 Samuel 19:2 – "abide in a secret [place], and hide thyself"

Psalm 20:2 – "Send thee help from the sanctuary and strengthen thee out of Zion"

Psalm 63:2 – "To see thy power and thy glory, so [as] I have seen thee in the sanctuary"

Psalm 68:24 – "They have seen thy goings, O God; [even] the goings of my God, my King, in the sanctuary"

Psalm 77:13 – "Thy way, O God, [is] in the sanctuary: who [is so] great a God as [our] God?

Psalm 96:6 – "Honor and majesty [are] before him: strength and beauty [are] in his sanctuary".

Meditations – 2

Inner man – Having communion with a living God in the secret place; affects our whole life.

Psalm 51:6 – "thou desirest truth in the inward parts: and in the hidden [part] thou shalt make me to know wisdom".

Romans 7:22 – "For I delight in the law of God after the inward man".

2 Corinthians 4:16 – "we faint not; but though our outward man perish, the inward [man] is renewed day by day".

Ephesians 3:16-17 – "according to the riches of his glory, to be strengthened with might by his Spirit in the inner man"

Colossians 1:27 – "the riches of the glory of this mystery among the Gentiles; which is Christ in you, the hope of glory"

1 Peter 3:4 – "But [let it be] the hidden man of the heart, in that which is not corruptible.

Revelation 3:20 – "I will come in to him, and will sup with him, and he with me".

Meditations – 3

Inner strength – A) Absolute truth active within us. B) Fellowshipping with resident doctrine. C) Jesus loving us right where we are

Isaiah 40:28-31 – "the everlasting God, fainteth not, neither is weary? He giveth power to the faint; and to [them that have] no might he increaseth strength.

Job 29:20 – "My glory [was] fresh in me, and my bow was renewed in my hand.

Psalm 27:13 – "[I had fainted], unless I had believed to see the goodness of the LORD"

Psalm 51:10 – "renew a right spirit within me".

Psalm 73:15 – "My flesh and my heart faileth: [but] God [is] the strength of my heart."

Ephesians 4:23 – "And be renewed in the spirit of your mind."

Colossians 3:10 – "put on the new [man], which is renewed in knowledge after the image of him that created him."

Revelations 3:8 --"thou hast a little strength, and hast kept my word, and hast not denied my name."

Meditation – 4

The Altar — The place of offering, sacrifice and worship (Judges 13, Psalms 43:3-4, Isaiah 6:1-8, Romans 12:1-2)

Abraham's Five Altars
1) *The Altar of Promise — obedience (Genesis 12:5-7)*
2) *The Altar of Intimacy — prayer (Genesis 12:8)*
3) *The Altar of Returning — returning & repentance (Genesis 13:3-4)*
4) *The Altar of Possession — walk of faith (Genesis 13:17-18)*
5) *The Altar of Absolute Surrender & Trust (Genesis 22:9*

Building an Altar (Genesis 22:9, 2 Samuel 24:20-24, Hebrews 13:10)

1) *Making sacrifice to God denotes total dependence and reliance on Him.*
2) *Saying no to self and yes to God — in effect presenting one's self in submission to God*
3) *Building altars became a habit with godly Abraham, the "Friend of God" (James 2:23).*
4) *Building of an altar in the land was, in fact, a form of taking possession of it.*
5) *Worship of God in the new land expressed Abraham's faith in the fulfillment of the divine promise.*
6) *Abraham was, by building those altars, taking possession of the land.*

Abraham's commission from God (Genesis12:1-8, 13:18 & 22:9).

Meditation – 5 Devotional Life:

1) *The result of hearing and seeing the reality of who God is and how he moves (action from thought and imagination) HEARING a Personal word*

2) *A word from God that inspires us to follow after him and a revelation of His devotion to us.*

3) *Mere knowledge turns to rhemas. The cross crucifies knowledge, there is no uncontrolled knowledge based by sight or natural reasoning. Faith only knows God.*

4) *Communion –A breaking of the bread and eating his life— Jeremiah 15:16; John 6:63-66*

1 Samuel 3:9-10 "Speak for thy servant hears"
Deuteronomy 18:20 "speaking from another source – death"
Isaiah 50:4 – "tongue of the learner"
Matthew 8:8 "speak the word"
Act 27:22-25 "As God said – be of good cheer"
Romans 12:1-2 "conformity / transformation"

Psalms 23
He is our: Possession, Provision, Peace, Pardon, Partner, Preparation, Praise, and Paradise.

Meditation – 6

Silence – concentration produces a muzzling of the outer life

Numbers 9:8 – "Stand still, and I will hear"

1 Kings 19:12 – "after the fire a still small voice."

Psalm 107:29 – "He maketh the storm a calm, so that the waves thereof are still."

Isaiah 30:7 – "Their strength [is] to sit still."

Psalm 50:21 – "These [things] hast thou done, and I kept silence".

Ecclesiastes 3:7 – "a time to keep silence".

Isaiah 15:1 – "Brought to silence."

Isaiah 41:1 – "Keep silence before me, O islands; and let the people renew [their] strength".

Jeremiah 8:14 – "Why do we sit still? For the LORD our God hath put us to silence"

Lamentations 3:28 – "He sitteth alone and keepeth silence".

Amos 5:13 – "Therefore the prudent shall keep silence in that time."

Amos 8:3 – "they shall cast [them] forth with silence."

Habakkuk 2:20 – "let all the earth keep silence before him."

Acts 15:12 – "Then all the multitude kept silence".

1 Corinthians 14:28 – "let him keep silence in the church; and let him speak to himself, and to God."

1 Thessalonians 4:11 – "Study to be quiet".

Revelation 8:1 – "there was silence in heaven about the space of half an hour."

Meditations – 7

Quietness is an Inner calm because of surrender and submission. A Pose of mercy.

2 Chronicles14:5 – "The kingdom was quiet before him".

Job 3:26 – "neither had I rest, neither was I quiet; yet trouble came"

Job 21:23 – "being wholly at ease and quiet".

Psalm 107:29-30 – "Then are they glad because they be quiet".

Proverbs 1:33 – "But whoso hearkened unto me shall dwell safely, and shall be quiet from fear of evil".

Isaiah 32:18 – "and in quiet resting places"

Acts 19:36 – "ye ought to be quiet, and to do nothing rashly".

Meditations—8

Inner rest – Delighting IN what you do, in a constant state of renewal.

1 Chronicles 22:9 – "Behold, a son shall be born to thee, who shall be a man of rest".

Job 34:29 – " When he giveth quietness, who then can make trouble? "

Proverbs17:1 – "Better [is] a dry morsel, and quietness therewith".

Ecclesiastes 4:6 – "Better [is] an handful [with] quietness."

Isaiah 30:15 – "In returning and rest shall ye be saved; in quietness and in confidence shall be your strength".

Isaiah 32:17 – "The work of righteousness shall be peace; and the effect of righteousness quietness, assurance forever."

2 Thessalonians 3:12 – "that with quietness they work."

Meditations—9

Inner Stability releases Divine Power—Ephesians 1:18-21 (5 forms in Greek)

Kratos: *Gods Manifested Strength*
Dunamis: *Gods inherent strength, His ability*
Exischuo: *Gods full strength going beyond*
Energeia: *Gods operative or energizing power*
Ischus: *Gods actual Power*

9 780615 727981